Linda

May These poems
add to your wonder!
Best Wishes,
Anne Brent

IN THE NAME OF WONDER

More poems by Armand Brint
Schools of Light, Linwood Publishers, 1995
The League of Slow Cities, Tenacity Press, 2001

IN THE NAME OF
WONDER

POEMS

ARMAND BRINT

Haley's
Athol, Massachusetts

Haley's
488 South Main Street
Athol, MA 01331
haley.antique@verizon.net
800.215.8805

Armand Brint
www.armandbrint.com

International Standard Book Number, 978-0-9626308-8-0
        trade paperback

International Standard Book Number, 978-0-9626308-9-7
        eBook

Cover and interior photographs by Armand Brint unless
otherwise credited.

Copy edited by Mary-Ann DeVita Palmieri.

For Franny

"Won't you come into my garden?
I would like my roses to see you."
—Richard Brinsley Sheridan

Contents

(continued)

Mercy for Monsters

Dino and Kong Sculptures, Gualala Trading Company & Nursery
Gualala, California • 2011

Creature from the Black Lagoon (1954)

We all know what it's like
to want to be left alone—
to sit in a rubber suit at the bottom of a lagoon
lost in a sweet, wounded reverie.
We do not want to hear
the propellers of a large boat
churning the water black
nor listen to insipid cocktail music
drowning out the incomparable sound
of bullfrogs.
We all know what it's like
to breathe the water of mixed emotions.
And who has not, at least once,
felt himself to be that fish out of water,
hating his own iridescence under the moonlight?
We all carry vestiges of the Paleozoic past,
when girls whispered behind our scaly backs.
And we were clumsy and inarticulate
on land—
constantly waiting to be rescued
by our mothers or the liquid glide of dreams.
We wanted to rebel, hide in a cave,
copulate with the hourglass
of our immaturity.
We just wanted to be left alone
to read Salinger and to grow our feet.
But the hunters were afraid of the dark and the deep.
They wanted to gut us
and toss our bones to the alley cats
that patrol the boundaries of this world—
the ones that keep monsters at bay
and wayward boats from puttering over the edge.

We all know what it's like
when our habitat begins to shrink—
when predators with their scalpels and
intoxicated rumbas suck the green out
through the straw of their pitiful lungs.
But even if they force us back beneath
black water,
we will return again and again
from the lagoon
of unresolved sequels.

On the Death of Fay Wray
King Kong (1933)

Oh, no, it wasn't the airplanes. It was beauty killed the Beast.

Fay finally fell from
the skyscraper of this life.
It was the Beast that killed beauty . . .
the beast of time and the accretion
of too much hoary experience.
The burden made her totter and fall
like some great, inarticulate ape
from the Empire State Building's spire
of celluloid and insensate steel.
She never asked for the role
of cowering in the massive hands
of a virgin's nightmare.
She never asked to scream through the bowery
of a prehistoric jungle or confront
the wild, almost human face
of transcendental fear.
She did not ask
to be the lone woman
on a ship of unshaved actors
and hot lights.
O Fay, we watched dumbstruck
as the trees crashed down around you
under the urgent light of a hungry moon.
Hoping we could unbind you in time,
we tried to stop our ears
against the fevered drums,
tried to make sense (for you) of the
incantation . . . *KONG, KONG, KONG* . . .
But we always failed.
And you, poor girl, were spirited away

to a household of bones and chest-pounding.
We watched in a black and white trance
as you swam nearly naked
in the great dark pools of his troubled eyes.
We watched him snatch you
from your taffeta hotel suite.
We watched in horror
as he scaled the granite and glass of sheer instinct.
And you were so blond and fragile—
waving above the city of tenements
like a flag of surrender.

The National Enquirer . . .

. . . singled out my home town courthouse
for possessing the top paranormal
event last year.
A motion-detector camera captured
a ghost floating down a hallway.
One janitor said, "I saw a dress walking by
in high heels!"
Enquiring minds want to know
if the spirit
received a particularly harsh sentence
at the courthouse
or witnessed some grisly scene there
or simply liked hanging out with those
on a fast track to the next world.
Maybe she enjoyed haunting lawyers
or, like so many others,
was a shimmering mist—
all dressed up with no place to go.
In any case, courthouse employees
seemed blasé about metal detectors going off by them-
selves
and night elevators stopping at every floor
without any passengers.
They seemed to intuit
that the courthouse stands between two worlds:
rich and the poor,
seen and unseen,
possessed and dispossessed.
I feel a kind of pride
knowing the courthouse ghost
put my home town
on the protoplasmic map

of the metaphysical.
And if you're wondering
about the tabloid's also-rans,
they're the same tired bunch
that part the veil every year
in order to feel a little jolt
of human recognition:
a Sasquatch sighting, Atlantis landmarks,
tears from a statue of the Virgin Mary,
strange beasts shot by Texas ranchers, and
a forty-five-foot creature on Lake Okanagan.

Tao of the Wicked Witch of the East
Wizard of Oz (1939)

I watched my sister's toes curl
like those bugs that ball up
when they die.
I watched not so much with grief
as with desire . . . for those shoes.
After all, according to the unspoken code,
I was next in line—
not some upstart from a world of gray tones.
I was brought up in the patrician East
where witches were taught to respect tradition,
polish their apples
before they injected the poison,
tend to their belladonna and hemlock
in neat rows,
out of noblesse oblige
take time to scare
even the most humble children.
And we were taught a beautiful cursive
for skywriting.
Those ruby slippers
are the perfect conductor
of earth's currents.
But when I try to take what is mine,
all I get is a handful of painful sparks.
And this girl, Dorothy, is so stupid,
she keeps a dog as a familiar.
I have a right to be angry.
I will mobilize my army of winged monkeys;
I will avenge my sister, and
I will feel the malicious glitter of those shoes.
No pink bubble of a witch

nor Wizard nor menagerie of weak companions
will keep that ... that pig-tailed girl safe.
I already possess the power of air and fire.
I only need earth
to complete the dark trine.
Then my broom shall sweep them all away.
Let them have dominion over water.
I will not fear liquidation.
Let their souls float on an ocean of tears.
Let them revel in the element
that seeks the lowest places.

The Wolf Man (1941)

Even a man who is pure in heart and says his prayers at night may become a wolf when the wolf's bane blooms and the autumn moon is bright.

When the Wolf Man comes
I will be ready.
I have inoculated myself
against the lycanthropic light
of the full moon
and applied silver polish
against its invisible burn.
I have swallowed tincture of wolf's bane,
and in the darkness—
its sharp white petals
open me like a steel trap.
When I hear his snarl at the forest edge,
I do not panic.
For I have walked blindfolded
through the mists
of the Carpathian Mountains,
memorized movie dialogue
until I shine like celluloid
in the moonlight.
When the Wolf Man approaches,
he comes slowly
laboring against my absence of fear.
I take my time turning to face him.
I've prepared for years
like a monk
in the tight cell of my body.
I've clipped my nails down to the nub,
shaved my head, slept on the hard floor
of lost opportunities.

But on that fateful night
when I finally look into his obdurate eyes,
I do not see the gaudy costume of his hate,
the penumbra of gypsy campfires,
nor even the moon in sheep's clothing.
I see only a man
who went to bed one night
cradling his litany of hurts—
and woke up utterly changed.

I Walked with a Zombie (1943)

There's no beauty here—only death and pretense.

Or maybe she walked with me.
By the time our marriage dissolved,
we were both the walking dead.
We could have used a voodoo priest,
but instead we hired warring attorneys
who made us broke
on top of being dead.
We walked under a full moon,
but our eyes were empty.
Our will had vanished
inside one another's contempt.
We walked through the island cane fields
of Saint Sebastian.
And like the saint,
we were pierced by arrows.
We were both saint and sinner
in that vacant night—
wounded one another so often
our bodies leaked out light.
We did not speak to each other—
our blood turned cold
inside the bone of our silence.
We were dead to one another
though we continued to sip coffee,
answer mail, and watch mindless television.
At night, we held our stiff arms out
as if reaching for something forgotten.
But we were dead tired and
merely shuffled off to our separate beds.

The Mummy (1932)

You, among all the monsters,
are most puzzling—
you trail your bandaged bones back through time—
vibrating under the nexus of a pyramid.
Your very existence demonstrates
there are at least three sides to every problem,
including death.
Your mouth is heavy with the dust of hieroglyphs,
and you answer every question
with the riddle of silence.
You are the stuff of Rosicrucian nightmares
as you walk stiff-legged on the knife edge of a curse.
Even though you hold the pedigree
of an old film canister,
you're relegated to the lower echelon of monsters—
the ones who must prove themselves
again and again,
the ones who must walk the earth
in search of an audience.
You started the craze
of storing one's heart in an earthen jar—
wrapping the body in bandages
as if the vagaries of death were more arduous than life.
Your eyes are even more deeply set than Karloff's
staring out from an ephemeral strip of film.
Of all the monsters,
you seem to have the fewest grains of free will.
You are as hollow as a windless flute.
And yet ... wasn't it love that brought you back
to Egypt disguised as a modern?
Love—
the one thing that might outlast the credits—

the reason other monsters trip you in the cafeteria
and nail your loose bandages to the bedpost.
You just gaze past them as if they were a mirage.
You do not share their bloodlust.
Bound in a kind of swaddling,
anxious to be reborn alongside your Queen,
you've come nearly full circle.
You, at least, believe in kismet—
while all those other monsters
march in lock step under an insatiable moon.

Attack of the 50-Foot Woman (1958)

She is the one who throws her shadow
over the football field of adolescence.
She is bigger than a billboard for Macy's lingerie,
bigger than the drive-in of teenage hormones.
She is Kali, destroyer of bad marriages,
mother of cyclones.
Her trailing hair is unfathomable—
her silhouette swallows the moon.
She wears her pituitary gland
on her sleeve,
and her heart is as large as a red sports car.
But I'm getting ahead of myself.
If we want to understand the 50-Foot Woman,
we must go back to the beginning,
back to 1958,
when everything lies half submerged
and therefore twice its normal size.
This is where she comes
upon a spaceship in the desert.
Its inhabitant somehow causes her to grow ...
grow beyond her drinking problems,
grow beyond the straight-arrow propriety
of Nancy Archer.
She becomes a thunderhead of rage—
a giantess squashing the life out
of her no-goodnik husband, Harry,
and Honey, his tight-sweatered mistress.
She keeps her 50-million dollar inheritance
and her enormous wardrobe.
But it doesn't stop there.
The 50-foot Woman becomes a force of nature,
a mythic presence in the shadow land of the '50s.

She absorbs the energy of 50 maenads
after a bacchanal.
She passes into the imagination
of a generation of girls who admire
and fear her ...
who drive through the desert
constantly checking the rear view mirror
for falling stars.

The Invisible Man (1933)

When I arrive home in the lowering dark,
my son has already left to get pizza with friends,
the dog is sleeping, the mailbox holds a few
anonymous bills, and the paperboy has forgotten
to deliver the *Daily Journal.*
I've hardly spoken to anyone,
as if the day were a long corridor
sound-proofed with empty egg cartons.
Leaves have begun to drop from the birch tree.
I feel like the neighbors can see clean through me,
so I close the venetian blinds.
The evening news is devoted to war
and young men blown out of their supple skin.
I have the odd sensation that I'm moving through water
like those translucent fish balanced by the tiny ballast
of their spinal columns.
On days like this,
I'm a mad scientist (as in angry)
whose experiment has gone terribly wrong.
No one misses me
unless I leave the room in a huff.
I'm a domesticated chameleon
blending in with the wallpaper.
And worst of all,
women stop sneaking furtive glances in my direction.
My leaves have begun to fall.
Soon, nothing will be left but a trunk
and an empty valise.
This is not the famous emptiness of Buddhism.
This is the curio cabinet in the corner
so preternaturally familiar it's no longer seen.
This is the invisible man

sold in hobby shops to distractible children
who may never take the poor fellow out of his box.
And if they do,
they'll likely leave him without a spleen.

Them! (1954)

This is an ode to irradiated ants—
but first a few ground rules:
when I say *you*, I mean the collective you
that scurries about in encoded formations
beyond our most advanced science.
The common term, *ant*, will have to stand in
for all the subtypes represented
by your gazillion ancestors.
And in this poem, you will be filmed in shades of gray
because the kind of color processing
required to depict fire ants is just too darned expensive.
Way back when, the studio was so flummoxed by your behavior
they simply called you *Them!*
as in anything other than us.
And for most of the kids of my generation,
the compound eyes in your big heads
made you a perfect proxy
for the morphology of atomic mishaps.
Each irradiated collectivist ant
could crush boulders in its jaws
but could not breech the enclaves
of our free enterprise system.
Let's face it, you were just the fevered metaphor
of some inebriated screenwriter
who hatched you one lonely Hollywood night
as he railed against dialectical materialism.
After that, you were all outfitted in the same dull exoskeleton
as if the politburo had assumed control over central casting.
Your giant identical bodies streamed over the landscape
as if hillsides were merely corrugations
of cast off cigarette packs

and you snatched up pedestrians as if they were grains of
sugar.
And yet, the hidden nests of your indoctrination
were finally vanquished
in accordance with the Illuminati Code of B movies.
You were summarily rooted out
along with the other irradiated creatures
surviving at the margins of our private picnics.
After all, we were us, and you were them!—
a bunch of worker ants
willing to hitch your mandibles to any exploding star.

The Phantom of the Opera (1925)

A monster is married to its fate.
It cannot see the grass
on the other side of the graveyard fence.
Take the Phantom of the Opera—
hiding in the catacombs
beneath the Opera House.
Not even Bizet at his most sublime
could fill in the craters of his ruined face.
Not even Christine of the alabaster voice
could transport him to the seashore
for a holiday.
And when she dared to unmask him,
one could hear falling chandeliers
shatter the Parisian night.
He looks out upon the world
through a thin film of acid,
drifting through his days like a cold asteroid
across the dark mirror of space.
Sometimes he thinks his exile is a dream.
He knows he was born to bask
in the pink light of society's praise.
But then pain returns to his abominable face,
and his overture becomes ponderous and oblique.
He has a premonition that the piano's teeth
will soon turn against him.
But he cannot stop his actions.
He is inked to his fate
like notes on a page of music in a minor key.
He wears the tragedian's mask,
and he will not cease until the curtain
smothers the ember of his unforgiving face.

Frankenstein's Monster
Frankenstein (1931)

When you see a cottage tucked
under the protection of an oak or
visible just above a thatch of cattails,
it might be worth a moment's pause
to listen for the hermetic sweetness
of a violin or
sniff the greenish chimney smoke
twined with the admixture of a fat cigar.
For your own dear monster
may have led you to a place
in the middle of a wood
just as Frankenstein's inchoate creature did.
This could be the very patch of sun
where you first learn the meaning of
"friend."
It is here that you first
sense the potential
of your ravenous heart and
begin to feel the shape of your yearning.
Under the oak's shade
you discover the power
that comes from naming things.
You feel the weight of the world
begin to lift from the axis
of your brutalized shoulders.
All your life
you've struggled to make sense
of your body—
to cast off the feeling
that you've been stitched together
out of spare parts.

You've dropped innumerable stones
down the well they call the soul
without hearing any of them strike bottom.
But in one moment—in this clearing—
you feel your life joined to the lives
of the greenwood.
And as you sit in the long grass
listening to a lilting violin,
you even begin to feel
some warmth for your creator.

Boy in the Bardo

Rocket Ship, Todd Grove Park
Ukiah, California • 2012

Gemini

My son moves between two worlds
weighed down by his bass guitar,
backpack, and bag of clothes.
His mother got the house and the dogs.
I live in a trailer in the country
with his pet rat.
It is up to him to maintain an orbit
around these double suns—
a lesson greater than his pre-algebra
or heavy electric bass.
Of course, we do what we can
to help him
through the gravitational pull of love,
but he's the one
who must shoulder the burden of transit.
For the most part,
he has memorized the stars,
steered clear of the exploded star
of our marriage.
Sometimes he pulls distractedly at his hair—
a sign of free-floating anxiety,
a sign of weightlessness.
And I know beneath his silence
he longs for the terra firma
of a single household
with a large backyard
and the sound of his sheep dog
before she got sick and died.
But he has to learn to oscillate,
to individuate and re-combine and
make it all so seamless he fools himself
into believing he is living one life.

He must devise his own pledge of indivisibility
amidst various allegiances.
None of this is easy for a twelve-year-old
struggling with that other planet of puberty
and the glittering green nebula
of girls hanging like mistletoe
in the depths of space.
He was born under the constellation
of The Twins. This is his lesson,
and now he must learn it.

Juvenile Hall

Once when my son was young,
he mistakenly referred to Juvenile Hall
as "Jupiter Hall."
Now he is spending the night
in Jupiter Hall.
I imagine him dressed in an orange jumpsuit
like the stormy orange brow
of Jupiter.
I cast my mind toward him,
but, confined to the single cell
of his universe,
he seems millions of light years away.
He rises in the west—
mispronouncing the sixteen moons
of his defiance,
and despite his size,
he spins with the velocity of adolescence.
I ask you, Father Jupiter,
to father me so I may father
the distant planet of my son
who even now floats in the difficult
atmosphere of his karma.
When our kids are young,
we never guess they'll risk themselves
beyond the orbit of our vigilance—
that we'll see bars instead of stars
in their caged eyes,
or that they'll lose their native twinkling
on the Milky Way of opiated country roads
and the exigencies of hormones.
But my son no longer spins the malapropisms
of childhood.

Instead he traces the razor wire
wound around the darkening sky
above Juvenile Hall.

Climbing the Tulip Tree

Two kids climb the
huge tulip tree
on the courthouse lawn,
a sight that would normally
make me smile—
except I just spent two hours
in the bowels of the old stone building
keeping my son company
while he waited for his hearing.
The petals are pink and other-worldly,
and the kids seem content
to stand suspended in the branches
waiting for the afternoon
to pass in a flurry of flowers.
They do not fear the adjudication
of sun and sky
and the aroma of the tulip flowers.
But my son holds his boyish face
in his anxious hands
surrounded by the gray skin tones
of those who would cloud the world
in cigarette smoke.
Even the walls are stained
with the disappointments of people
who started out as tree climbers.
My beautiful son stares at the discolored linoleum
that absorbs the heavy footsteps
of petitioners who come here every spring.
I suppose I should be thankful
for a tree
that provides a brief haven
for the unencumbered bodies

of children
who fall so slowly
that we hardly notice
their descent.

Hot Tub

Last night,
my son positioned himself
In the hot tub
between two girls.
I could hear them giggling
and talking over one another
while I tried to sleep.
I listened to the steady burbling of jets
as if I held a stethoscope
up to a case of uncorked champagne.
I was getting angrier by the minute
while they were getting . . . .well,
happier.
I kept thinking about them
disturbing the neighbors
and my need to wake up early the next day
for work.
But they were busy
creating the bubble of their freedom.
Here was the bright line
between middle age and youth,
the shining circumference of a hot tub
under the early stars of spring.
Finally, just as I was getting out of bed
to tell them to leave,
they rose from the tub.
The young have an uncanny sense of timing
down to the last possible moment
of grace.
Of course, my son and I
exchanged harsh words
after the girls had gone home,

which made me feel even grumpier
and less inclined to sleep.
It was a school night, for Pete's sake,
I was just getting over a virus,
and I was in the midst
of the chronic condition of middle age.
But my son didn't care about any of that.
For one brief interlude,
he'd luxuriated in the middle of heaven
without the requirement of a harp
or even a backlog of good deeds.

Bus

I feel numb
even though it's my son
who's taking the drugs.
He is on a bus that doesn't stop
at Winnemucca or Albuquerque or
any city on the map.
His only rolling stops are made
at drive-through kiosks
on the astral plane of addiction.
He must have spent his allowance
on an open-ended ticket
through the high deserts of dopamine
where the sun sets
in colors not found
on any automobile association map
showing the way home.
When he was a child,
I found comfort
in the cartography of his gentle eyes.
I used to sing to him,
"The wheels on the bus go round and round . . ."
but the wheels have come off the bus,
which nonetheless keeps rolling
through the synapse of ghost towns
and dust devils with their Stetsons pulled down.
These days, I think about seedy Greyhound stations
and shudder.
There are places that reek of lapsed hygiene
and lost compasses.
They deal out diesel fumes
through the long tailpipe of discarded dreams.
He is on a bus without a destination,

a train without a station,
a body without a sensation.
He sleeps with his face pushed against
a greasy window of stars.
And he wakes in the mountains
outside of a Flagstaff
that isn't there.

Tattoo

A tattoo is a true poetic creation, and is always more than meets the eye.

—V. Vale and Andrea Juno

For his eighteenth birthday,
my son wants a tattoo—
three nautical stars
inked to the underside of his arm.
I'm not so keen about these stars
shedding their uncertain light
on his unblemished body.
I suppose this is a statement
about creating his own night sky
out of their small luminosity.
They are, after all, nautical stars
designed to guide him on an ocean
that already laps up
the pastel shores of his boyhood past.
Or maybe he's creating his own religion
of adulthood
with its trinity of watery light.
I think he wants to make his mark
on the epidermis between the worlds.
And, of course, to imprint his stardust
on future girls.
I am concerned about penning
indelible choices
before he even learns the constellations
of his own making.
And I am unsettled by birthdays that begin in pain.
But as the old song goes,
he wants to embrace his manhood
by swinging on the needle point of a star ...

carrying moonbeams home
in a translucent jar of possibilities.
He sorely wants to impress
with the indigo of those five points,
one for each of the cardinal directions
and one for the unknown.

In the Name of Wonder

At daybreak, a clergyman thought he heard groans ... as he walked along the top of the dike. Bending, he saw, far down on the side, a child apparently writhing with pain. "In the name of wonder, boy," he exclaimed, "what are you doing there?"
"I'm keeping the water from running out ...."

—*The Legend of Hans Brinker*
Mary Elizabeth Mapes Dodge

For the first time, I speak
to the recovery group about my son.
I feel self-conscious,
naturally—
what parent wouldn't feel
the room closing in
as he struggles to find words
to compete with the doggedness
of addiction.
My voice quavers,
the dam threatens to burst,
but I keep the proverbial finger in the dike—
that same finger that has so often
smoothed my son's hair
or pointed out the Big Dipper
so that he might know
where to replenish his soul
on a dark, clear night.
I think he has temporarily forgotten
the constellations.
He just moves from one dark room to another
where the walls are water-stained
and no one cares if dopamine
floods his brain or not.

He and his friends are too busy
sticking a finger in the eye
of their own pain.
I am the only man in the group,
so I feel somewhat caught
in the fishbowl of feminine witnessing.
I wonder if I can measure up
to the women who are more practiced
at unburdening themselves
to a higher power
in the surprisingly secular meeting room
of the Calvary Baptist Church.
They have already reclaimed their puckered fingers.
But I'm a newcomer.
Once I begin,
it's not hard to speak about my child.
After all, what could be more natural
than to ponder all that dammed dark water.

Spending the Holidays in Jail

My son seems adjusted to the fact
that he and his cell mates
will have to come up
with their own makeshift Christmas.
He said they'd concoct something
from the commissary—
a junk food potpourri to indulge
during lockdown on Christmas Day.
It's a hell of a way to spend the holidays.
Yet, I'm amazed at how philosophical he becomes
when there is no place to run.
He uses his time to read novels,
do pushups in his cell, and
reflect on the barbed wire hole
he has dug for himself.
My son and the inmates on Wing-4
plan to make a holiday spread
by crushing and mixing uncooked Ramen noodles,
powdered sugar donuts, and candy bars
in a thirty-gallon black plastic garbage bag.
Not exactly s'mores around the campfire
or even roasting chestnuts,
but it's something to do while he does his time
in an upper dorm of hell.
I don't know why the judge
gave him such a stiff sanction
for a first infraction;
I guess he's trying to teach him a lesson.
There are no chimneys in jail—
no Santa in a red jumpsuit
to compliment my son's green one.
No one to bail him out

from the isolation of his own North Pole.
No, I'm afraid this year
my son has landed squarely
on Santa's "naughty" list.
I don't think he really expects
much more than an extra dollop
of cold mashed potatoes
sitting on his dinner tray
like a lump of coal.

All the Way Home

I remember hearing about trees
able to produce exotic new fruit after grafts
and bespectacled tree surgeons
perfecting their bedside manners
under the shade of apple boughs.
So when the hand surgeon mentioned a skin graft
to address my son's third degree burn,
I wasn't completely undone.
I just hope my son can continue
to use his pinkie to experience
the subtle realms of human reach.
He doesn't seem too concerned
as he holds his gauzy hand above his heart
to reduce the swelling.
I have a whole fistful of reasons why
I didn't phone back the imperious surgeon.
But mainly, it's because the jail nurse
was supposed to make the call.
Maybe she's not attuned
to the individual personalities of the fingers.
Or has forgotten
that each part of us holds memories
of a happier time.
Or doesn't understand that these anemones
close at the slightest provocation.
But a finger is like a little soul
feeling its way through the undulating world.
And the last digit
is kin to the foot's pivotal pink piggy
that waits while its brethren
stroll off to the market
or fill up on roast beef.

It shivers in the cold under thin wrappings—
so that when its time comes,
it can produce a great cathartic squeal
all the way home.

Eureka

Last night, my son and I
endured a 6.5 earthquake
exactly equal to the seismic displacement
between us.
It happened in the town of Eureka.
When it hit,
we were pulling into a Target parking lot.
No kidding. First we thought the car
had suffered multiple flat tires
until we noticed all the other cars
shaking and wobbling.
The industrial light stanchions in the lot
swayed like palm trees in a mean storm.
And overhead, a chevron of geese flying south
suddenly wheeled to the north
and then began flying in circles
as if their collective compass had gone haywire.
I had to weave my way
between emergency vehicles
in order to get my son
back to his residential facility on time.
I rose early the next day
to grab breakfast at Renata's.
They were playing Sinatra's
I've Got the World on a String ...
which seemed somehow appropriate.
The trembler appeared on Page 14
of the *San Francisco Chronicle*,
but I don't fault the editor
for burying Eureka's falling masonry
on the back pages.
Earthquakes are old news in San Francisco.

The editor's relationship with his son
may not even show up on the Richter scale.
They probably share weekly dinners
where they discuss Herman Hesse.
But my son and I were at the epicenter.
I'm just happy we survived the quake.
Happy a tsunami didn't take us
just as we were regaining our balance.
And now I wonder if this sudden upheaval
might somehow relieve the tectonic pressure
between us.
And suddenly I feel an upswelling of joy.
Maybe that's why the city is called Eureka.

Hell on Wheels

My son flipped his car
trying to avoid a deer
on a back road outside Geyserville.
Thank God, my son survived unscathed
as did the deer.
But the car was wrecked.
Truth be told,
I hated that shiny blue demon.
It always stank of drug deals
and low self-esteem.
Under its custom body
and industrial speakers,
it was just a simple four-cylinder.
But it had the look of easy money
and bad women.
It was too much sizzle
for my rural progeny—
too overreaching and too profane
for the honest rules of the road.
There was no courtesy in the thrum
of its mufflers.
That car turned my son
a reptilian shade of blue.
The whole idea of that car was trouble.
We should have made a U-turn
the first time we saw its grillwork.
But the devil is in the detailing.
I think that deer
was sent from the back roads of heaven
to save my son
from the soulless machinery
of sex without love.

And now the car's twisted frame
sits smoking in a junkyard.
One can clearly see how it thrived on
burned out streetlights and
potholes of oily rain.
One can imagine how the dark engine
of its narcissism
was content to idle under the hood.

White Pickup Truck

When I saw my son's new white truck,
I thought about white birds
skimming the turquoise water
of possibility.
When I considered the four-cylinder engine,
I narrowed the list down
to more compact birds
with better mileage.
This is as close as a young man
is likely to come to flight.
This is the bird that teaches one to consent
to the small spaces
that crowd everything out
except the sheer joy of sex—
which is to say a full tank of gas
on an open road.
The new truck parked across the street
looks accustomed to the hard work
of beating its wings.
It also looks effortless.
It looks as pristine as a bird on a wire.
This is the first time
my son has come right out
to say he believes in flight.
This is my son's way of saying
love is possible.
He is poised to pick up
the disparate pieces of his life
in his white pickup truck.
And he has parked his intentions
across the street
where I can supply my small blessings

from the front stoop.
It is my son saying yes to the sky
and the sea and the earth of every day.
It is a seagull, a petrel, a dove . . .
it is all of the above.

Home on the Range

Last night
my son slept in the cab
of his small pickup
in the WalMart parking lot
in Williston, North Dakota.
Trading a portion of sleep
for the illusion of safety,
he parked under a light standard.
I can picture his truck
strategically parked in the middle
of the Great Northern Prairie.
He says the people
are generally good natured,
though many, like him,
hungry for work in the oil fields.
This morning
he'll start looking for a home
under the big cloudless sky
where the ghosts of buffalo still roam.
He'll begin swapping
his dystopian California playlist
for the cowboy song
of his new life.
I can picture him on his palomino
silhouetted by the rising sun,
summer brown grasses waving
good-bye and hello at the same time—
adios to the kid
who crossed the liminal Rockies—
hello to the fella
whose features are just beginning to form
in the blue morning air.

I Found a Cigarette Butt and It Reminded Me of You

I found a cigarette butt,
and it reminded me of you.
It was next to the camellia bush
outside the back door.
I know this is not the greatest way
to begin a poem about missing someone,
but it's true.
You were very good about smoking outside—
not so good
about disposing of the crumpled filters.
I just sent you an electronic cigarette
that delivers nicotine
but only emits water vapor.
I have to admit that it's a little hard
to imagine you using it
at the glowing tip of North Dakota's oil fields.
Oh, well. It was a good thought.
And now snow is about to erase
the line between Canada and the US.
I hope you will save your cigarette money
to buy warm clothes.
You've only been up north for a couple of months,
but it's the difference between summer
and winter.
Forget about fall. That's just a half-smoked cigarette
left in the slush.
You need to fix your fuses.
Haven't been able to drive around at night
for six weeks.
What can I say? You're twenty-two
and starting a new history without headlights.

Well, we all start out in the dark.
At least the light of a cigarette
is something. I understand that.
And I'm not asking that you be illuminated
by the aurora borealis every night.
Just asking that you have working headlights
and learn something from the snow
about internal light—
so you can stop smoking.

Feeding Two Birds with One Scone

Olives and Red Willows, Saracena Winery
Hopland, California • 2013

If you stay in the same place long enough . . .

. . . you come to know its span of highway.
You know the hairpin curves
marked by their stations of the cross.
You know the exact color of the lupine and poppies
that grow next to makeshift memorials protecting drivers
from ghosts of the deceased.
You know which service clubs
have adopted which sections of road,
and you keep tabs on the amount of litter
that accumulates on each.
You memorize the little fenced-off pasture
where ponies graze,
as if it were a diorama from a children's book.
And you feel blessed
every time you catch a glimpse
of the mythical white deer.
You know the dry creeks and decrepit bridges
named after minor dignitaries from the last century.
You wonder at ramshackle roadside barns
that still retain a hint of red.
You know where the black and whites
set their speed traps
and where the guardrails abruptly stop.
You have twenty-nine different words for fog.
And sometimes, on a clear night,
the crescent moon becomes a poem by Rumi
that takes your breath away.
If you stay in the same place long enough,
you develop gratitude for the orange-clad workers
who come to clean up the orphaned trash.
And over time, you come to accept
the sharp punctuation of skunk

and stretches of highway
that invite turkey vultures to swoop down low
over the broken bodies of carrion.
And, too, there are places where vacant bodies
vanish into vapors of twilight
or into the radio's resurrected melodies.
If you stay in the same place long enough,
longer than anywhere else, longer than longing itself,
you begin to imagine the landscape
without this highway, this old weathered highway
that you have almost come to love.

Cows

All night long, cows have been lowing, snorting,
wailing, bellowing, blowing, and belching
like some deviant brass band incessantly tuning up
but never dropping into a melody.
I don't know why they're so agitated.
But I wouldn't want the milk from this night.
I used to enjoy the sound of cows
like fog horns mapping the distance—
something plaintive, almost soulful about their calling
under clotted clouds of twilight.
But tonight they chew on the cud of my sleep.
Like dogs barking across the hillocks,
they infect one another
with their undomesticated fear.
The cows are moaning to their sister moon
under the Milky Way,
and in my sleep-deprived state,
I think that if I repeat the word *cows* enough times,
the large, loud syllable of these animals
will fade into meaninglessness and silence.
But at four A.M., an asylum of cows persists
outside the porous walls of my trailer.
They are scraping their hooves
across the blackboard of night:
a cacophony of clumsy, clamoring, confusticating,
cantankerous, anti-cows—
their cow-bells clanking like mistuned glockenspiels.
These are not Old MacDonald's obedient cows
or Gainsborough's daubs of quiet color
but cows with heavy udders and pendulous moods.
Slowly, begrudgingly, I begin to understand
these beasts cooking fear in their four stomachs,

letting it circulate through the massive chambers
of their milky hearts,
filling the sac of their bucolic lungs,
shaking the great cage of their bodies,
letting it percolate up
through the obtuse bones of the skull
and over the pink pasture of tongue
until every square acre,
down to the hoary tail,
erupts in a bovine lament—
which is to say, a plea for serenity,
the familiar scent of apples and earth,
and not much else.
Every once in a while, silence descends
like the aftermath of a temple bell—
then night churns again with cows,
cows that in the buttery light of morning
will lower their big heads into grass
and forget entirely about what had them so upset.
I try to consider their enormous need for peace
as I listen for the train whistle of my lost sleep . . .
though soon, I know, I'll have to grab a cup of coffee, black,
and heave my slow, cumbersome body
off to ruminate over my own worrisome field.

Sticky Fingers

Did you hear about the Quebec maple syrup robbery?
It's about to turn the black market
a lovely shade of amber.
I didn't even know there was
an underground demand for maple syrup
until a spokeswoman
announced the concerns of the
Global Strategic Maple Syrup Reserve.
This worried woman did not speculate
on how someone might fence all that hot syrup.
But under harsh television lights
she looked like a maple that had been over-tapped.
Canada is up in arms
over the theft of a sweetener—
while stateside we've become accustomed
to hate crimes and schoolyard shootings.
Of course, our northern neighbor
honors the maple leaf on its flag
while we project the bars
and cold stars of our individualism.
Maybe we could curb violence
by replacing Old Glory
with the emblem of a cider apple
from Johnny Appleseed's common stock.
The news clip of the maple syrup caper
shows where the robbers squeezed
through a bent-back chain link fence.
It looked like something a couple of teenagers
would do on a dare.
It makes me wonder if hungry teens
also stole a truckload of buttermilk pancakes.
In any case, the syrup burglars will,

no doubt, be brought to justice,
as their fingerprints are smeared
all over the enormous Formica countertop
of their shame.
Meanwhile, sap continues to rise
in the sugar maples allowing our breakfasts
to remind us
not to take any drop of sweetness
for granted.

River Lights

My friend plans to kayak
just after moonrise.
As she dips her paddle
into the water,
she'll release liquid lights
from tiny dinoflagellates—
their small agitations
causing phosphorescent ripples
under the moon of her quiet awe.
Surely each person has the capacity
to turn up the lamp of the body
when night is clear
and the waxing moon throws its arm
around our blue shoulders.
In my mind's eye,
I already see her
gliding inside a halo of dark water—
the only sound a haiku
of paddle meeting tremulous river.
The water is full
of what scientists call *bioluminescence,*
and the ocean—a few hundred yards away—
is filled with light.
Even plankton add their small wattage
to the blue heaven beneath our dreams.
We are all fireflies
caught in the jar of our limitations.
And yet, we glow.

False Spring

During these warm weeks,
birds gorge themselves on pyracantha berries—
sometimes flying into our office windows.
They're so drunk on nectar,
they forget about clear divisions
of space.
They forget about the natural order
of mortar, glass, and feathers.
They are drunk and flying free
the way we do in our best dreams.
Every so often, we hear a thud against glass,
and we know another bird
has filled its hollow bones with drunkenness—
tried to crash the stolid world
of office workers.
Our only question is,
how powerfully has it failed?
Usually the little fellows remain stunned
for a moment,
then hop unsteadily away—
the way we might if we'd missed the curb
and landed heavily on our spectacles.
In a flash, the world can turn,
one second flitting through pine dapples,
the next lying in the bushes,
little pinioned stars circling overhead.
Someone, God maybe, should have told them
about the perils of false spring,
about winter in sheep's clothing.
This is the time
when the magnolia by the courthouse
blossoms in such pink profusion

that the accused feel certain of acquittal.
This is the time
when our hearts are pierced
by the arrows of random valentines
and our sap rises to the dangerous cusp
of the pelvis.
This is the morning of daffodils
and the evening of drunken birds.
Yesterday, we discovered a broken bird
beneath the window,
a testament to this false spring.
It lay in the bushes—wings outstretched—
as if it were flying over the River Lethe,
as if it had negotiated its barrier of glass,
as if its feathered soul had escaped
in one great drunken burst.
Scientists might explain the sudden flexion
of the dead bird
in the language of brainstem lesions
and spontaneous muscle movement
at the moment of death.

But when I look down,
I see that it has already flown away.

I believe all dogs go to heaven . . .

If having a soul means being able to feel love and loyalty and
gratitude, then animals are better off than a lot of humans.
— James Herriot

. . . even when they drool
over the doilies of their domesticity.
They are bound, eventually,
for the Elysium that rewards loyalty
with the pure white bone of eternity.
They follow the scent of companionship
to a place where mild breezes
are caused by the continual tail wagging
of their kin.
And all their coats shall be lustrous
and all their days filled
with the rabbit of pure release.
They go where harps play
at a pitch only they can hear.
And every bone is buried
in the effulgence of a cloud
where it glows like a hydrant.
All dogs ascend to the topiary of heaven
where ancestors are immortalized, mid-leap,
amidst columns of Arcadian Milk-Bone.
They roll in the smell of the long-dead—
making snow-angels in the powder of the hereafter.
Dogs circle three times in the long sheaves
before they curl
into the unmarked territory of sleep.
And when they wake,
a flutter of butterflies leads them leaping
through the butter-shine
of blue fields

to a breakfast of clear water
and a large meaty bowl of gravity.
For heaven is also a place
that smells like spring—
a place to lie in the shade
of their own contentment
and remember the smell of earth
after the first rain.

Fin Whale

The largest whale is so huge,
it embodies its vast namesake:
blue.
Next in line, the fin whale,
floats like a sentient isle,
a self-contained paradise
blowing bubbles from the champagne
of its musical soul.
Dead maybe two weeks,
one particular female fin
washed up on a Westport beach.
Death does not seem to diminish her
to crowds who come to commune with her carcass
so wholly out of proportion
to our daily cares.
But there are a dissolute few
who carve graffiti into her largess—
a few who hack off chunks
from the enormous imagination of her body.
We are the only species
who make souvenirs of the dead,
scratch our finite names
into the infinite undulations of the sea
made manifest.
While Buddhists sit in the charnel grounds
meditating on death,
others fail even to recognize
its saucer-sized eyes staring at them
from out of the void.
In fact, one group
tried to drive over the whale's flukes
but got high-centered and stuck

up in the cold air of shamelessness.
They abandoned their pickup truck
as they will some day
abandon their own damaged bodies.
For even the deep, abiding whale knows
it must surface
and that eventually "all that arises
passes away."

Twitter

Twittering should be left to the province of birds—
those beings that sift sunlight
through the scrim of luminescent wings.
These are the ones that sing for their supper,
their sex, their religion of blue air.
No digital device in the universe
can compare to the sound of a thrush
at twilight
or the secret chittering in the lilacs
above a stone birdbath.
Hand-held devices
are simply another way to block out
the Dawn Chorus.
They do not bless us
with their arrogant screens,
ironic ring-tones,
or compact shells
stolen from the transistor radios
of our youth.
A backyard songbird
feeding from a blackberry bush
is a hundred thousand times more interesting
than a clumsy email beeping
from a Blackberry machine.
These gadgets send out pulses
like lonely buoys in cold troughs of waves:
they blink to life
in the existential space between cell towers.
These devices wear the pixilated death mask
of the hyper-real:
they tweet without a scintilla of love.
It's important to remember

how we once surrendered to the pantheism of summer
and invoked Thoreau
under a pond of wheeling stars.
It's important to pay homage
to the holy solemn miracle of spring.
And it's important for all the reasons beyond our knowing
to leave the winged, hollow-boned, feathered, migrating,
iridescent, elegant, soaring, epiphany
of chirping, peeping, twittering birds ...
to their own devices.

Black-Crowned Night Heron

The black-crowned night heron
stands motionless on a lava rock
protruding above the hotel koi pond.
Very occasionally, it will pick off
one of the small orange fish,
but mostly it watches.
The heron has been accepted
by the hotel staff as one of their own.
It comes to work,
creates a little bubble of concentration,
and eventually flies home.
The black-crowned night heron
is unabashedly exotic.
And yet, hunched over the koi pond,
it seems as ordinary
as a security guard at a shopping mall.
Large koi drift across the pond
unperturbed—
while the heron waits.
Perhaps it stands
upon the stone of Sisyphus
that has settled in a green pond
of unassailable fish.
The heron holds the koi
in the pool of its black eye.
It spends a good part of the day
watching the sun glint
off the chrome bodies of fish.
Its hunched posture
suggests someone who will never
own the car of his dreams.
One might mistake

the black-crowned night heron
for a statue—
except its look of unrequited hunger
is so familiar.
Standing on its stone,
it looks like someone perched on a sofa
watching a test pattern of fish
on late night TV.
Koi glide across the pond
but never enter the heron's
black-crowned dreams.

Watershed Defined

...that area of land ...within which all living things are
inextricably linked by their common water course and where,
as humans settled, simple logic demanded that they become
part of a community

—John Wesley Powell

I live in the Orr Creek watershed
where kids smoke pilfered cigarettes
under municipal bridges.
And deer peruse rose gardens
inside the white noise
of Saturday night stock car races.
It's just a fraction of a zip code
defined by the lazy circle
of a single turkey vulture.
It's a lozenge of light
on the picnic ground of symbiosis.
The Orr Creek watershed
includes blackberry bushes
that border the neighborhood dog path
and dogs
that relieve themselves
in the meager blackberry shade.
It's the sheltering canopy
of martyred leaves
and a community composed of seventy percent water
and thirty percent single-family dwellings.
It's the dream that descends
from the nimbus
of our collective cloud.
It's the raccoon family
that drinks from the creek
until their rings turn blue

and the crows that scan
for anything that shines.
It's the glistening aftermath of snails.
And the communal sound of rain.
It's the cadence of a ballgame
coming from a neighbor's radio.
And the moon shedding
its watery light
over my own backyard.

McDonald's

Until today, I hadn't really noticed
that the McDonald's near the freeway exit
had suddenly vanished—
just two empty arches leading to a vacant lot.
Now that I think about it,
even the scraped earth left behind
seems an improvement
over the fast food façade
with its supersized plastic tubes
fit for giant hamsters
rather than human children.
I hadn't noticed it was gone
because it always seemed
a box of dead space
inhabited by the slightly rancid odor
of overwrought French fries.
What a blessing it would be
if all things McDonald's
simply disappeared like old socks
or bad dreams.
Ronald McDonald could be retired
to the home for misguided clowns.
And the charred Golden Arches
could replace the entrance to Dante's Hell:
Abandon all hope ye, with an appetite, who enter here.
I once saw a depiction
of McDonald's franchises
as little pinpoints of light
inside the dark map of the United States.
Some urban areas were so densely packed with Micky Ds
they looked as if they were on fire.
And now our local McDonald's has disappeared

like the mists of late summer
or adipose slowly burned into oblivion.
They will build a new one soon.
But for now,
we get to glimpse the world
the way it used to be
when hamsters were free to burrow
and children played sandlot games
under the invisible arches
of their own golden natures.

Bees

Bless me into usefulness.
                              —Buddhist Blessing

A trailer truck overturned
in Wyoming
busting open two hundred honeybee hives.
Clouds of bees
stopped traffic in both directions.
The bees were probably already upset
by the unhappy motion of the truck,
and now they were overturned, homeless
and swarming along Highway 220—
searching for their queens
and the pre-fabricated palace of their hives.
The newscaster said, "Here's a story
that's getting a lot of buzz,"
which just goes to show how unfeeling
the news has become.
Even under the constant threat
of colony collapse, these bees
had resigned themselves
to an unnatural itinerant life
laboring in commercial fields.
But now they were stranded
on the highway,
sideswiped by a pickup truck driver
who probably never brought his wife
a bouquet of flowers.
The bees looked on
as workers in yellow suits
burned their broken hives.
I imagine the remaining bees
would not last long

in the cold Wyoming night.
And if they did,
their honey would be bitter.
What we need is news
from the queen-dom of the wild,
where bees are free to flower
to their tiny hearts' content.
We need to paint the yellow lines
with buttercups
and stay alert at the wheel—
for thousands of lives
may depend on our wakefulness.

Hummingbirds are attracted to red . . .

Hummingbirds have forgotten the words
                                                    —graffiti

. . . and that's why hummingbird food
is the same unnerving color
as maraschino cherries.
The red dye is most likely toxic,
but manufacturers know
that it will attract hummingbirds
as well as human impulse shoppers.
The other thing I've discovered
about hummingbirds
is that the alpha males chase away
their scrawnier brethren.
This behavior does not exactly correspond
to the benign, almost other-worldly image,
so often embroidered on blouses
or fashioned into tiny wind chimes.
But the cheeky little hummingbirds
could care less
about maintaining the integrity
of our metaphors.
They like the color red, damn it!
And they like to brawl
and get drunk on sugar-water.
Their wings move
faster than the human eye can see,
so that they seem to levitate
like little yogis.
They're probably considered
the philosopher-kings
of their little red universe.
But the truth is—

they prefer honeysuckle
over our prefabricated feeders.
They'll condescend to come to the porch,
but their sixth hummingbird sense
allows them to bring their blessings
mostly when we're not watching.

Song

Male mice sing
when they detect the scent
of a female mouse—
not just sounds
but song patterns,
like tiny whales serenading
their paramours
through the mysterious
ocean of high frequency.
It appears mice
belong to that small band of creatures
that sing in the presence
of the opposite sex.
They join songbirds, porpoises,
humpback whales, insects,
and possibly bats
floating on a little ark of song
through the silent deprivations
of the natural world.
Scientists want to dissect
the brain behind those songs.
They're searching for clues to autism
and other human ailments.
If mice could talk,
I think they'd say the cure is easy:
more song.
But we'd rather court
our women with lattes and muscle cars.
We'd rather spend our days
wooing them from behind computer screens
than crooning the ballad of love.
I salute the little lab mouse

whose nose begins to twitch
when his Minnie saunters into a maze.
I applaud the one whose heart
suddenly bursts open in song.

Donkey Crossing

On the lava desert
north of Kona,
a yellow sign says:

DONKEY CROSSING NEXT TWO MILES
DAWN AND DUSK

The wild donkeys are wise;
they know to cross the highway
only during the hours
when humans are most
like animals themselves
and, therefore, less likely
to be occupying their cars.
Alongside the highway,
high school sweethearts
have spelled out their initials
in white stones
against the dark pumice.
And in the distance,
coconut palms mark a glide-path
of green light
all the way to the sea.
Everything is held in balance
between this world
and the other.
Equus africanus asinus
survive on scrub brush
and small pockets of rain water.
They commune
with the wild clouds
that darken in the afternoon
of the donkeys' sleep.
And somewhere

out on the lava fields,
wild donkeys wait
for white stones
to come alive
under a twilight moon.
This is their signal
that it's safe
to cross over.

Jukebox Heart

Garden Statue, Mendocino Botanical Gardens
Fort Bragg, California • 2012

Thanksgiving

We are flying to Los Angeles for Thanksgiving—
borrowing the air from sacrificed turkeys
that wish they were doves.
We are flying south
in the near winter of cramped airline seats
to the City of Lost Angels—
flying back to our mothers
above a mantle of haze.
We are throwing a shadow across LA,
descending toward our long tables of earth
to reminisce about the heaven of childhood
and the gravity of distance.
We are about to look for angels
in the Lost City of the past.
We are flying above the turbulence
of old misunderstandings
and broken wings—
above the turkey's vacant, luckless,
angelic body.
We are flying to the City of Lost Families
brightening the air like angels.
We are flying to Los Angeles for Thanksgiving.
But it is that poor doomed bird
confused by rain,
carrying a soggy heart
beneath its formidable wishbone,
that turkey of giving—
unable to fly farther than a flutter,
wishing it could escape like a dove—
that deserves our thanks.
It is that butterball of myopic flight
under its halo of false starts
that leads us home.

She Sighed When I Said Philology

We discovered erogenous zones
in euphonious phrases,
had that epiphany about language as intercourse,
tangled the sheets of journals
in the heat of articulation.
We became athletes in pursuit of multiple origins,
explored one another's most intimate etymology,
deflowered common usages
and unearthed Latin roots—
all of it suspended in the libidinous soup
of cross-fertilization.
We massaged each other's iambic feet
with the lavender oil of sonnets.
She loved the size of my vocabulary,
I marveled at her phonics.
We performed cunnilingua and
brought stars on to the blank page of night.
We mixed metaphors with abandon
then cleaned our linens
in the pure sunlight of good editing.
She read the dictionary of my body;
I quoted Strunk and White over the economy
of her shoulders.
We deep-kissed French syllables
behind the tongue-and-groove bookshelves
of irrepressible libraries.
We took the words into our pores
until our skin shone with literacy.
We strolled down the boulevards—
an open book —
in the naked sans seraph font of love.
Strangers scrambled for their reading glasses

as we passed by.
We lived in that afterglow
when a poem lights the candle of the body.
We lived on another planet
where the weather speaks in villanelles
and anapests of rain
alliterate against the wet window sill.
And we created a bedroom of new sonnets:
our enjambments sped past the vigilant line;
our couplets exploded on a singular rhyme.

Chicken Tamales

My wife uses a rock
to weigh down husks of corn
in a pan of cold water.
The words, "thank you,"
are etched into the otherwise smooth gray surface
of the stone.
She is making tamales
for her daughter's boyfriend's birthday.
She fills the husks of gratitude
with *masa*, chicken, garlic, and onion.
And she also makes them
for Elijah's Mexican sister
who sits in the empty kitchen chair
under an invisible shawl
sipping the strong coffee
of the other world.
My wife is a softener of husks—
and in sympathy, my body relaxes.
I hear the comforting sounds
of kitchen utensils
speaking their singular squeaky incantations
over the constituents of tamales.
She is going to use her new mixer
to metamorphose the cornmeal
into something fit for the avatar of birthdays.
And as she prepares the ingredients,
she also thanks the gods of manna and *masa*
for the fecundity of the earth
and for the birthday tamales
that will line up like sleeping candles.
Finally, the tamales lie radiant
in their little hammocks of corn,

glazed in the green light of chili peppers.
The saint, on her seat of power,
smokes the husk of a cigarette
as if she is contemplating an important decision.
And after a long moment,
she raises her wine glass
to signify her approval.

I am just putting my ex in the freezer . . .

. . . when the doorbell rings.
It's two neighborhood girls
searching for their lost black cat.
When they leave, I have to start the spell
all over again—
write her name on a slip of paper,
put it in a plastic bag,
fill the bag halfway with water,
seal it, put it in the freezer
with a prayer
wishing her well and wishing her away
from my life.
This is not
a-black-cat-at-midnight-under-a-full-moon spell—
simply an untangling
through the white magic
of the Frigidaire.
Sometimes people get lost.
Even when you send two angels out,
they don't come back.
Sometimes people crash
into the iceberg
of each other's sorrow.
I hope she is safe, avoids freezer burn,
and navigates her ice floe
into some happiness under the aurora borealis.
I hope the freezer
allows her to meditate like water
sitting in full lotus
in its little tray of self-possession.
Sometimes in the middle of the night
I wake to the sound of the refrigerator

humming past the graveyard of my marriage.
It is waiting to anchor the kitchen
of a new day.
Sometimes I feel my ex
like the loss of some frostbitten extremity.
Anyway, I wish her a warm parka
and an endless thermos of coffee.
And I hope the girls find their cat.

Dia de los Muertos

In this season of the dead,
my wife arranges orange marigolds
in a blue teapot.
Gossamer ancestors
are drawn to color.
They kick piles of fall leaves
which may or may not react
to the swinging of their spirit feet.
We are never wholly alone.
Just the other night,
my relatives visited me in a dream.
As far as I can remember,
they were all chatting amiably
as if they did not have a care
in this world or the next.
And sometimes my father sits next to me
on a park bench.
As time is not important,
he does not rush to judgment.
We sit and feed spirit pigeons.
Maybe a leaf moves.

Why I Get Haircuts at the Beauty College

It's not just because the haircuts are cheap.
It's also because the students are tentative and earnest.
They touch one's hair as if it were a gift.
The young women are just beginning to learn mastery
over balding middle-aged men
who come in for a little off the sides and back.
They are learning the beauty
of a good bedside manner.
Students practice applying make-up to themselves
between haircuts.
Most of them overdo it,
but the extra paint can be forgiven
within the confines
of this secret temple to Aphrodite
with its little swiveling altars.
And the excesses teach them
to protect themselves with the lacquer
of hair gel and cosmetics.
They are practicing the metaphor of hard candy.
Yet most students retain the glow of youth;
their cheeks still suggest a hint of apples
even under blush and harsh lighting.
The Ukiah Beauty College
is, as much as anything, an homage to youth—
which is always beautiful, albeit skin-deep.
Though the building smells old
and full of chemicals,
something lovely animates the place.
And even though these students are learning
to twist hair
into the fetish of a French braid,
something hormonal and young and beautiful remains.

In the parking lot,
it's all diffuse winter light and cars that need washing.
But within the inner sanctum of the college,
one sits draped in the barber's chair
like an acolyte,
staring into the vast space above cubicles
where great golden gears and gleaming wheels
turn the starry cosmos of Beauty.

Danke Schoen

My heart says danke schoen (last line of the last chorus)
—music by Bert Kaempfert
—lyrics by Kurt Schwaback and Milt Gabler

Over a breakfast in bed
of blueberries and crushed pineapple,
I think about Wayne Newton
singing "Danke Schoen."
I don't know why Mr. Newton's
penciled mustache and pompadour
come to mind.
But there he stands outfitted in sequins
under the spotlight of the Stardust Hotel.
He milks the song for everything it's worth:
"Danke Schoen, darling, danke schoen,
Thank you for all the joy and pain . . . ."
For a brief moment,
the song seems to capture
the entire human experience.
It's essentially a happy song,
even when weighted down
by Germanic melodrama
and layers of pomade.
The scene is so vivid,
I can hear slot machines
in the background
offering meager breakfasts
in their little spinning windows of fruit.
And I can smell curlicues
of cigarette smoke
adding their own blue light
to the oversized neon lounge of Las Vegas.
When I listen carefully,

I understand that the song itself
recounts a medley of sweet moments
even if they are fleeting.
And though the song is wistful,
it avoids regret.
In that sense, it is big-hearted.
And now Wayne opens his glittering arms
for the final chorus,
and I'm singing right along with him:
"Danke Schoen, darling, danke schoen . . ."
because the song has become a kind of blessing
for everything that has gone before
and led to this spotlight of sun
in our happy, flamboyant bed.

My First Tattoo

When I walked into the tattoo parlor,
I thought I'd found the place
where all dissolute, misshapen, alienated,
rejected, and oversexed cartoon characters
went to drink themselves to death.
Various semi-naked knockoffs of Bettie Page
seemed to lick their inked-red lips
at the virginal canvas of my unsuspecting skin.
Needless to say, I thought I'd gotten off at the wrong stop,
but my strange dream bus was already grinding its way
through wet clouds above the narrow street.
Actually the grinding came from the tattoo needle
making its mad revolutions in the electric space
above my naked leg.
My tattooist said the first cut is the worst cut—
which became my mantra for the rest of the session.
The tiny inked incisions felt like they were being rendered
by some diabolical cross between a soldering iron
and a razor blade.
It wasn't hard to remember the First Noble Truth:
that suffering exists.
And so, I applied the nonattachment balm
of fearless tattoo breathing to the pain of my lower leg.
Soon, even the cartoonish characters
seemed to lose some of their malicious luster.
And the neon skulls, daggers, dragons, and devils
receded to their rightful place as mere decorations
in this floating world of tattoo parlors, wet streets,
and declining bank accounts.
Finally, my leg began to feel numb,
and I was able to ponder my beautiful damaged flesh.
The tattoo was a retirement gift to myself—

a way of reminding the animal of my body
that life remains wild and wholly unpredictable.
When the tattooist had finished,
I looked down on the new tattoo
of the Buddha sitting half lotus in perfect serenity
astride a bucking bronco careening its way
over the rodeo grounds of my inflamed right leg.

Prayer

I was taught to pray as an antidote . . .
so it was natural to crouch in the corner
of the junior high school boiler room
imploring the God of my fathers
not to let a tornado rip the school apart.
Turns out, the cyclone merely kissed
the school's corrugated roof
then lifted back into the miasma
above our heads.
We survived our adolescence
with its terrible weather of pimples
and the miserable climate
of unhappy households.
I prayed in the southwest corner
of the cataclysm of Kansas.
I wasn't even sure what I was seeking.
It was more like the prayer
an animal might make out of instinct.
At some point, I must have realized
that every decision we make
is a prayer of one kind or another,
but mostly we are saying
"I want to live,"
even when we know what living means,
even as we run headlong
into the heavy weather
of our ignorance or someone else's.
Lately, I have come to understand that
life is a prayer.
It does not take the great dark body

of a tornado
to recognize our fear.
But only a prayer can lead us
out of the boiler room.

I Send You Angels

I send you angels
from my mind,
flocks of them—
if that is the term—
to inoculate you
with their good intentions.
And I send you the Buddha
and all of his bodhisattvas
to surround you in the golden light
of the eternal now.
I send you sunlight
from my backyard
and a light breeze
rustling the plum tree.
And I send you
the sound of a piano waltz
just audible
from where I sit.
I send you the ordinary quiet
that allows angels to swing
in their hammocks of cloud—
the same quiet that issues
from the mind of the Buddha
washing away thoughts full of noise
and the anarchy of regret.
I send you the sparrow's song
which is small and powerful.
I even send you the sound
of the neighbor kid
practicing saxophone scales

inside the bubble of childhood.
And I send you
the single white butterfly
that just flew by.

What the Prophets Say

Faith is an oasis in the heart.
　　　　　　　—Khalil Gibran

Since marriage is a leap of faith,
we should ask those who have looked
beyond the bed of newlyweds
and studied piles of married laundry.
We should ask the ones
who have fashioned their prayer beads
out of grains of salt.
For they know how to keep the peace.
The wise ones understand
that we cannot make someone over
in our own image—
for we are not gods or goddesses,
nor do we understand perfection.
Better to wonder at the abiding decency
of the other
and water the seeds of goodness.
Those who stand at the altar
are advised to live simply as two people
willing to forgive one another in advance.
The sages know that when we are young
our beauty has just begun
to penetrate beneath the skin
where it is stored like sunlight in honey.
That is why when the sages make their matches,
they do not look for souls with flawless complexions
or ones who like long walks on the beach
or foreign films.
No. The prophets place kindness
at the top of their list.
I think the prophets would also say

"Carry an umbrella,
because sorrow is inevitable as rain."
And when you look down at your new wedding rings,
I believe the wise would say that you are looking
at the image of a halo.
Not because couples are destined to be saints,
but because that is what people wear
when they enter love's domain.
Finally, some would say
that marriage is an institution,
but the enlightened call it a blessing.

Dust Bunny Nebula

My wife scrutinizes a ball
of dust and fur
as if peering through a telescope
at some distant cluster of stars.
She is astonished
that this clump of cosmic magnetism
has attracted so many
specks of depilated life.
Our small home contains Whitman's multitudes.
It's a wonder we can even hear each another
across all the spent gamma rays.
The dog sheds, we slough skin,
and spiders spin their thin sensibilities
overhead.
Another world exists
of dust motes and ancient crumbs,
of words mumbled under one's breath
and barbed seeds
that cling to old clothes.
Memories float through sunbeams
like exploded stars,
and photos whirl around us
from the planet of youth.
Our dog lives in the present moment
of redolent socks
and the subatomic industry of ants.
We sip coffee in the microscopic detritus
of last night's meal
and peruse the front page news
which is fading fast.
It has taken sunbeams
eight minutes

just to reach our small kitchen . . .
and pass through us.
In the meantime, the dog begs
for a morsel of scrambled egg,
and with every whimper and wag
new worlds are born.

Full Moon over Coyote Dam

Acolytes come
to the top of Coyote Dam
to view the largest and brightest
moon of the year.
First we see a liminal glow
above the hills,
and then the full moon rises
as slowly as a great turtle
pulling itself over the lip
of the horizon.
My wife and I bring a bottle of wine
to toast the full moon
sending its shimmer
across the water.
One woman extends her nine-month belly
into the perigee of lunar light.
She is hoping, perhaps,
to start the tides of labor
on this clear night
above the glimmering of the lake
and the call of white geese.
Slowly the moon rises
until it is the only thing in the sky.
We sit on a bench
under this single incandescent bulb—
drinking wine and
thinking our secret thoughts.
Everything is pregnant with wonder.
The dam feels as if it's about to burst.
We try to read the moon glow

on the lake,
but it does not speak to us.
It speaks only to the woman
holding all that reflected light.

Driving in a Storm

Just to break up the monotony,
I chanced a quick glance
over to the opposite side
of the freeway.
Three Great White Egrets
stood amidst green stubble,
mustard flowers,
and rain growing thickest of all.
Their elegant bodies
looked like exclamation points
signifying the real world
that exists just beyond the freeway.
I couldn't resist
imagining them taking flight—
as symbols are apt to do—
over endless trucks
on Highway 5.
I'd have spent more time
musing over these slashes
of bright sentience
standing motionless in relentless rain,
but I had to return
to the business of driving.
And now, the three egrets
are many, many miles behind
standing on the edge
of my imagination.
I am surrounded by desolation,
but they seemed content
to think their fish-shaped thoughts
and take solace
under the white wing

of their one true song.
I thank them.
Even though they could not possibly know
what a difference they made
to this one poor driver
making a long road trip south
to visit a dying friend.

Meditating with Mosquitoes

A mosquito sings in my right ear.
It's a song of blood and hunger
that the mosquito part of me
truly understands.
Nevertheless, it is difficult
to meditate with mosquitoes.
They constantly draw you away from your breath
with their little grappling hooks.
The meditation room is as hot and humid
as a swamp,
a perfect breeding ground for the mosquito mind
which would rather suck blood from the present moment
than rest in silence.
I begin to visualize myself as a human bug zapper
arcing out frissons of hot blue light.
Then I realize this behavior goes against the precept
about preserving life.
So I imagine myself as a mosquito net,
which makes me feel claustrophobic
and stranded in a malarial jungle
with only a pen knife and a toy compass
to extricate myself.
Outside my ear, the high-pitched hum persists.
At this point, the mosquito has stuck its
needle-thin proboscis into the middle
of my meditation.
I decide to sing along in my mind
with the mosquito,
but I keep getting stuck on the word "calamine."
Then I imagine the mosquito
executing a difficult piccolo solo
in the corpuscular minor key of A Negative.

Even after all this effort,
I find myself swatting
at the tiny dentist drill
just beyond my right ear.
Still, some part of my mind understands
what the mosquito has been trying to point out
all along: that the breath—
which flows in and out of the ten directions—
contains enough space
to hold the entire insect kingdom.

Point Dume

My brother scatters the ashes
off Point Dume cliff
while I stand behind reading a blessing.
It is a glorious day
high above the Pacific.
Far below,
Hollywood is filming a commercial.
It has something to do with a couple
taking their wedding vows
amidst waves crashing on the sand.
There is a strange symmetry
between what is going on above
and below.
My brother is spreading his wife's ashes
over the incalculably blue water.
She is part of it all now—
even the film company below
that doesn't have the faintest idea
about what is required from a marriage.
The actors are only about the size
of ants.
But my beloved sister-in-law
is bigger even than Whitman
may have guessed.
My brother slowly lets the ashes
give shape to the wind.
It is a grim task
and yet unburdening in a way
that cannot be quantified in words.
Everything is distilled into itself:
blue sky, white birds, blue water.
My brother repeatedly sweeps his arm

out over the edge of the cliff
in a gesture so saturated with meaning,
it nearly defies gravity.
Finally, there is nothing left
but to make our way back down the cliff
where the crew is wrapping up its shoot.
When we look back from the parking lot,
Point Dume looks impossibly high
and far away.

I Ate My Wife's Still Life

She bought a few hard green pears
for a still life.
They were the first pears of the season,
but I was happy she'd found
subject matter
that wouldn't wander away
or change according to the weather.
Still, when the pears began to blush
into ripeness,
I was tempted.
And when the kitchen became redolent
with essence of pear,
I had to picture
my wife painting them in a green bowl
surrounded by fat purple grapes
and a few fall apples.
It was—I admit—pleasing to the eye.
But I began to feel that the pears
did not want their lusciousness
captured in watercolors.
I became convinced they would rather
turn black and mushy
than capitulate to posterity.
And then I thought about Dr. Williams
jotting down a poem
asking forgiveness from his wife
for filching those plums
out of the icebox.
And so, I ate one last night . . .
another this afternoon after lunch.
Perhaps it would have been better
if I'd eaten a less painterly fruit,

but in golden October light,
the pears were the very picture
of paradise.
And they tasted even better
than they looked.

Felicitations from the Floating World

Sunset
Redwood Valley, California • 2013

Statue of Liberty

Give me your tired, your poor,
Your huddled masses yearning to breathe free,
The wretched refuse of your teeming shore.
Send these, the homeless, tempest-tost to me.
I lift my lamp beside the golden door!
    — Emma Lazarus, inscription on the Statue of Liberty

She stands out in the blustery rain and cold
attempting to wave cars
into the Liberty Tax parking lot.
Her Statue of Liberty costume
consists of a toga-like smock
and a spiky green foam rubber crown
with matching torch—
the kind of get-up you'd see
on crazed fans at a pro football game.
I feel sorry for her,
as this has to be one of the town's worst winter jobs.
Aside from the unhappy spectacle of the endeavor,
it seems unlikely that tax clients
would just pull into the lot on a whim.
I can't imagine that tax preparation is prone
to patriotic impulse stops.
She must feel mortified standing in the rain,
engulfed in that ridiculous billowing outfit
as friends whizz by.
Given half a chance,
I'd guess this tired, rain-soaked teenager
would huddle
under the monument of her own statue—
yearning to breathe free
and be shut of this minimum-wage job.
Maybe it would be the *Statue of Carefree Summer Dresses*

or the *Statue of Sitting by a Cozy Fire While Reading a Book.*
I suppose some day,
she may look back on her degradation
and attempt to transform it into a work of art.
But for now,
she must assume the attitude of a statue
and ignore taunts and embarrassed looks.
She must shine her torch on those poor masses driving
into the tenements of their own lives.
She must provide a symbol of something
greater than the rain.
It is up to her now.
She must show the naysayers
what this country is all about.

Pulp Fiction Highway

The mortality of all inanimate things is terrible to me, but
that of books most of all.

—William Dean Howells

I heard just the tail end
of a radio conversation
about how unsold pulp novels
are transformed into filler for highways.
As a travel writer,
the speaker appreciated the irony
but must also have felt some regret
upon discovering that whole worlds
end up in a slurry of asphalt and aggregate.
I never realized how much thought
went into the composition of highways.
And it doesn't surprise me
that we drive over the deliberate plots
of old books
in an illiterate rush toward the denouement
of sales racks.
Who knew that the highway
included the low-brow machinations
of jilted lovers and lonely detectives?
Or that we could navigate a lifetime
of crises and redemptions
without ever leaving the car?
Apparently, there are noir streets in some cities
perpetually lost in shadows
and hard-boiled dialogue.
And there are towns in Texas
paved with nothing but laconic Westerns.
Some dreamy roads wind up and down hillsides
like the heaving bosoms

of Romance novels.
And we've all been on Sci-Fi roads
that stop in the middle of nowhere.
There are unrequited roads not yet traveled
and roads from youth
that spread out before us
like an open book.
The only other thing
I remember from the interview
is that some novels
are shredded into snow for movie scenes.
But that, dear reader,
is not the kind of weather
you should be driving in.

Elegy for Leaves of Grass Bookstore

When the bookstore closed,
I felt the dead-weight ballast
of all those unread books.
I felt the soul bruise
left by the ape grip of commerce.
And I felt the flaccid shadow of the next tenant
spreading over the store's open floor plan.
The lipo-massage spa will cater to the body not the brain.
Maybe the change represents some kind of balance
along the main artery of town.
After all, the bookstore kept its doors open for thirty
years.
Perhaps it's time for the Kali Yuga
of dubious wrinkle cream.
Anyway, we reminisced around a nicked-up table—
once reserved for sale books.
It was a kind of wake for Walt Whitman—
Word over all, beautiful as the sky!
The last thing we did,
before the owner flipped the CLOSED sign,
was to read letters from Ms. Aplet's fifth grade class.
Each child thanked us for donating books
so they'd have something to read
over the humid expanse of Chicago summer.
Most of the kids said that if they lived in Willits,
they'd help save the bookstore—
though they had only the vaguest shimmering sense of
California
and couldn't afford their own summer reading.
One girl said she'd cherish her new books—
make them into family heirlooms
passed down from generation to generation.

Proof that books have the power
to enshrine familial imagination,
transport kids to a small town in California,
and make them believe in a just world
willing to rescue shelves of unloved books.
One day, maybe these kids
will step into the adult summer of their lives
and remember the vellum and ink
passed down through generations of memory.
They'll feel a sudden, overwhelming affection
for their fifth grade teacher, Ms. Aplet,
and that bookstore sinking in the west
whose crates of books washed up
on the shores of Lake Michigan.

Barbie Dolls

Be wary of any enterprise that requires new clothes.
                                    —Henry David Thoreau

A friend of a friend's daughter said ten Barbie Dolls
had formed a suicide pact.
She didn't know when they were going throw themselves off
the top of the china cabinet
or arrange themselves behind the fat tires
of the family car,
but she was inviting her girlfriends over
to hold a kind of vigil.
Before they go, I imagine the ten
will want to pitch their tiny compacts
into the sea,
gorge themselves on pepperoni pizza,
and tell Ken to take his sexless body
off to the Tupperware convention in Sarasota.
These ten will want to make amends
to the tens of thousands of girls
who dreamed of tight plastic waistlines.
They will want to let their hair turn back
to the color of wet straw on a dark afternoon.
And they will want to ignore the panic of mirrors.
I imagine one of the Barbies,
the stewardess model perhaps,
tossing a cocktail match
into an oily pool of polka dots and polyester.
Every act of defiance makes them a little stronger,
a little more interested in the life of trees.
They keep postponing their pact
for one more sunset.
Finally the Barbies decide to sleep on it.
Some arise the next day as evangelists with new names.

Others become scholars of *Pygmalion*
or turn to Eastern religions or Sartre or drugs.
Maybe one or two attempt to go back,
but one of the girls, reading Thomas Wolfe,
calls out "You can't go home again!"
For all ten—whether they suffocate themselves
in chiffon or not—
Barbie is dead, her grave marked
by a bright pink handbag and matching heels.

Fortune Cookie

The fortune in the cookie says,
"You have an unusual equipment for success,
use it properly."
This might have been a message from Freud
instead of a mistaken transliteration.
Why do men always think about the equipment
packed loosely in their trousers?
And why does it always seem to bode
good fortune
even when it is clouded by hormones
of heavy weather?
Most fortunes can be misinterpreted
by the body.
In fact, there is even an old joke
that instructs diners to add
"between the sheets"
to the end of every fortune cookie fortune.
Perhaps that is why the cookie
always seems to be smiling.
Anyway, I don't remember what we ordered
for dinner that night
or what we carried home
in little white pagodas of cardboard.
But I was struck by the crinkled fortune
I have kept all this time
in a chipped blue cabinet
along with other mementos—
each conveying something
about the past
and perhaps the hermeneutics
of the future.
I like the fact that fortunes

travel inside these little packages
of sugar and vanilla.
Who can resist breaking open the stale shell
to find a pearl inside?
I've opened many fortune cookies
in my time,
but the only other one I remember
stated, "You will be getting a big supplies."
I just hope my equipment can handle it.

Oregon Motel

ATTENTION HUNTERS!
NO PLUCKING DUCKS IN OUR ROOMS
OR OUTSIDE IN GARBAGE CANS!

My friend encountered this motel sign
in a far flung corner of Oregon.
I have to wonder who would pluck his duck
in the place where he sleeps.
I suppose if a great deal of beer were consumed
or if the hunter was especially angry
at the poor duck
that simply became a feathered proxy
for all the daily indignities
suffered by the huntsman in the plaid cap—
it might, on a rare occasion, be understood.
But, apparently, it was common enough
to warrant a permanent sign.
Maybe the hunters thought they'd clean their birds
and furnish their lumpy motel beds
with a feather pillow all at the same time.
Two birds with one stone
comes to mind, but that proverb
doesn't exactly fit the crime.
Plucking ducks over a garbage can
in the parking lot
might be marginally better behavior,
but still does not rise
to the level of the explicable.
Why would anyone fill a rusty can
with the bloody-feathered bad medicine
that accrues from shooting a bird
at the zenith of its short life?
Surely, even a hunter who wears camouflage to bed

will fail to elude his haunted dreams.
Think of all the ducks through time
that might have lived out their iridescent lives
on quiet ponds and quiet skies.
All those birds that might have sailed overhead
into the good blue karma
of converted hunters
who no longer had a need
to attend to the dismal motel
of mortal signs.

One Candle

This is a note to the woman
in the dark restaurant booth
gazing at a birthday cupcake
with one candle.
I can almost see the ghost
of Edward Hopper
flitting in the shadows.
The restaurant buzzes with conversation
except within the little circle of light
where the year is passing in silence.
I'd like to wish her "Happy Birthday,"
but I am a stranger
from across the aisle.
Of course, it is winter.
There is light, but very little heat.
You might say
we are all living in the glow
of a single candle.
I don't know how to describe
the look on her face—
wistful, maybe.
I'd like to tell her
that there will be other cakes
with more candles
in her future.
But so many of my predictions
have fallen short.
Hopper never painted anything
without a modicum of light,
for how can you recognize loneliness
without a candle?

Valentine

Valentine, F. Latin, Valentinus, name of two Italian saints
whose festival falls on 14, February.
　　　　　　—Oxford Dictionary of English Etymology

Just after the annual prediction
that we will suffer six more weeks of winter,
Valentine's Day rolls around.
It's named after two Italian saints
who must have been martyred for love—
their hearts pierced by arrows
like the feathered graphite shafts
that adolescents draw on binders.
It seems these two
were responsible for teaching
how to cut the heart's dual shape
from a raw red page of construction paper.
And even more miraculous,
they were able to reconcile
the heart's warring halves
into a single prayer.
We will never fully know the lives of these saints,
only their perishable monuments
of flowers and chocolates.
Their contributions come to us now
through faded valentines pressed between the pages
of our personal histories.
And yet, it is enough for us to be blessed by love—
to sanctify the heart
with the simple implements
of scissors and paste,
to float on a white doily of innocence.
It is enough to make cut-outs
in the shape of forgiveness.

It is pleasing to picture these two mendicants
inventing the first valentine
from a pair of folded wings.
I imagine them strolling in a halo of Italian sun
or liberating gondolas of moonlight.
It is easy to see these two sons of Italy
predicting a beatific spring
amidst the shadow of winter.
And so, we owe our thanks to Saints Valentine
for illuminating the manuscript of love,
for the heaven of Eros,
and for the indelible heart
with its erasable arrows.

Poldi and Bibi's Last Anniversary

*Parrots, tortoises, and redwoods live a longer life than men
do; men a longer life than dogs do; dogs a longer life than
love does.*

—Edna St Vincent Millay

The precious metals
and jewels are exhausted
by the seventy-fifth anniversary.
There simply is no place to go
after diamonds . . . .
How do you keep the mystery alive
when the last anniversary symbol
expired forty years ago?
And yet this pair of giant land tortoises
has been together
since the invention of Edison's light bulb.
But after 115 anniversaries,
Bibi has become increasingly violent
toward her mate.
She even bit off a piece of Poldi's shell—
which is roughly equivalent
to wrecking a guy's 1964 Mustang convertible.
Maybe Bibi just got tired
of laying a century's worth of eggs
without even a single night of umbrella drinks
with the girls.
Poldi probably could have displayed
a little more affection,
instead of pretending to be a rock.
Even with a steady diet
of shuffleboard
and succulent aphrodisiacs,
zoo keepers cannot seem to foster

a rapprochement.
The two may yet find their way back
into one another's flippers,
but for the moment,
they've decided to give each other
a little space—
maybe see other turtles.
Bibi is already planning a cruise,
while Poldi retreats further and further
into his shell.

The Trouble with an Electronic Book

The trouble with an electronic book
is that you can't press a flower
between its pages
or sense distant sunlight
contained in its paper.
There is no pebbly cloth
beneath the dust cover,
no hard back
protecting the prose.
No faint scent of roses.
You could maybe stroke
a calico cat in your lap
while reading,
but it wouldn't be the same.
The trouble with an electronic book
is that it doesn't cause you to stop
and silently thank libraries.
You can't see, smell, hear, taste, or touch
its blessing.
An electronic book looks strange
next to a chipped mug of coffee—
like dancing with a robot.
It's a slide rule in a candy shop.
An electronic book is a tree
turned into a telephone pole.
It speaks to the circuitry of the brain
but not the heart.
And what is literature
if not the marriage of the two?
And what is a good marriage
if not something like the love
of a good book.

The world of books is round.
The trouble with an electronic book
is that its world is flat.

Returning from Hawaii

We arrive in the rain and cold
of San Francisco,
and we head home
behind a truck hauling caskets.
We travel through three time zones
and over the ocean of our resistance
to face the decidedly non-coconut-palm-lined beaches
of utility bills and dirty towels.
Our kitchen is totally devoid
of a Tiki Bar; our bodies lean
toward the reassuring sound of waves
that are not there.
The first night back,
I begin to grind my teeth again
in the existential confines
of the bed.
Don't get me wrong,
I love my home—
especially when it's an island
in the middle of pacific feelings.
But sometimes it's hard to leave
the giant sea turtles
of another land.
I'm sure the Hawaiians
are ambivalent, at best, about the haoles
that arrive on their shores.
And I'm sorry about that.
But sometimes it's hard to leave
a deep redolence of flowers—
even if they had once been colonized
without a sense of wonder.
Traveling home can feel claustrophobic

especially in the rain and cold
behind a casket carrying truck.
Perhaps this is comeuppance from
the gods of the tropics.
And yet, everywhere we look
we see hibiscus,
and our skin stays alive
with its fierce tattoo of sun.

Beach Boys

The Beach Boys urgently ask,
Do you, do you, do you, do you, wanna dance—
do you, do you, do you, do you, wanna dance . . .
in falsettos
as pure as the moonlight
that suffuses their song.
I imagine a lifeguard tower
that might be mistaken for a gazebo
and the sound of waves
spending their youth against
the cool white sand
of a popular beach.
I'm guessing the girl
wants to dance as much
as the boy,
but her diction is better.
She's learned to distrust boys
who swallow their consonants.
But the boys can't help falling
into a pleading kind of slang
confronted by the girl's bare arms
and the phallus of the lifeguard tower
outlined by the moon.
Their falsettos cause
stray beach dogs to howl,
and yet they reach for harmonies
achieved only in the crucible
of teenage yearning.
Wave foam is insistent
and moon white
against the dark water of adult sublimations.
But by this time,

they are both bathed in the light
of their own hormones
and working feverishly
to translate the song
into the language of the body.
The slow dance lasts only a few dreamy minutes,
but they leave the beach
in a state of perfect locution.

When Hell Freezes Over

An awful lot is going to change
when hell freezes over.
Think of all the things
consigned to a dependably infernal hell.
For example, hell would have to freeze over
in order to finally get that deserved
promotion/apology/settlement/
building permit/kindness from in-laws/
winning lottery ticket/etc.
Now imagine snowmen with carrots for horns
and little goatees of black ice.
Consider brimstone caves
suddenly frozen into stalagmites
and icicles hanging
from burnt out slag heaps.
Of course, there will be a lot of sinners
whose tongues are stuck to frozen light poles.
And it will get dark early.
Things will be different.
All those notions that we thought
could not, in our wildest dreams, come true,
will manifest inside the cold nimbus
of our disbelief.
The check will actually arrive in the mail,
airports will be fun again,
politicians will earn our trust, and
Murphy's Law will be repealed.
When hell freezes over,
cynicism will take the shape
of carnivores encased in ice.
And we will skate
over their prehistoric bodies.

Bells will ring out
over a month of Sundays.
Every moon will be blue with serendipity.
And in the clean, snow-glistened air,
pigs will begin to fly.

New Arrivals

The lower shelf
of the "New Arrivals" cart
is filled with books on bondage,
submission, fetishes, erotic fairy tales,
and the like.
Someone has emptied the entire
secret compartment of their library
into the dirty light of the used book store.
It makes me wonder if the owner
had given up his or her S & M interests
for butterfly collecting
or sweeping beaches with a metal detector
or spelunking.
The store proprietor must feel
there is a market for used sex—
especially on a lonely Saturday night.
Patrons usually bring in mysteries or romance novels.
But these new arrivals
are more like hard-bitten mysteries
who handcuff romance novels
to the bedposts of a basement bedroom
away from the curious gazes of the literary shelf.
And the no-nonsense non fiction books
must look aghast at these scandalous volumes
as if they'd just arrived off the boat
from a small Eastern European country
of unorthodox sex.
It's true they speak in a dialect
unfamiliar to the rest of the store.
And they stick out a bit like a sore thumb
or a rope burn in a pile of silk.
Soon they will be exiled

to the ghetto of "Erotica,"
alphabetized next to "Existentialism"
at the back of the store.
There they will wait beneath their stained covers
for new owners.
They will wait in the reflected light
of other used books.
They will wait with their spines slightly bent
and inflamed from over handling
and learn to like it.

Welcome to the 'Hood, 2012

The young guy on the corner
spins a sign advertising five-dollar pizzas
while the convenience store down the street
sells single cans of malt liquor
to early risers.
People heading north pass through the 'hood
on their way to the redwoods
or horseback riding
or to the clean scent of snow.
But first they must pass
through the tetanus gates
of a four-way stop
with its boarded taco stand
and the industrial musk
of a hulking tire store.
The best kept lawn
belongs to the mortuary;
otherwise the neighborhood
has turned prematurely gray
in anticipation of the nearby freeway.
The orange pizza placard spins like a warning—
it's a sign of the times
announcing the apocalypse.
Each stop sign stands for a Horseman,
and each Horseman stops traffic
waiting for entropy and cheap beer
to do its work on the 'hood.
Many pass through this threshold—
there's nothing remarkable about it
or about the deli that sells cheap hand guns
alongside dill pickles
or about the motorhome

selling oversized beach towels,
lurid decals, and statuettes of Elvis
playing his cement guitar for the oncoming traffic.
Hardly anyone notices.
Hardly anyone notices the neighborhood turning to ash.
Perhaps this is the prophesy
foretold so long ago by Egyptians, Mayans
and all those visitors from outer space.

Heartbreak Hotel

*"American entertainer died today at his home in Memphis Tennes-
see. The cause of death was capitalism."*
                    —*Pravda* (Soviet Union News agency)

He died twenty-five years ago today—
sitting on the john
reading a book about the Shroud of Turin.
His heart, swollen with sequins,
simply stopped.
On this twenty-fifth anniversary,
thousands descend on Graceland.
I drive out to the monastery
to contemplate how to shake loose
from this broken record of birth and death,
the one where Elvis sings "Return to Sender."
On this anniversary day,
wildfires up in Oregon turn the sun red,
shining like a spotlight
on this stage of smoke and desire.
We wait under the dry ice of a Vegas sky
for Elvis to sing a medley
to our resurrected youth.
The sky is on fire,
but he does not appear
except in black and white snapshots
from "Jailhouse Rock."
There are the famous smirks,
the high cheekbones, the unruly hair—
fragments gone back to earth and
particulate-heavy sky.
Fans remember where they were,
what they were doing,
and how their shoes turned blue

from the shock and sadness of his passing.
Some say he never died.
Elvis sightings are as frequent
as bleeding images of Jesus.
They do not know
that even the thrusting pelvis
arises and passes away.
They do not know
that we are born into this *Hotel*
where the *Heart* is meant to *Break*.

Poem That Starts Out Morose But Ends on a Happy Note

We are entering
the provenance of Christmas
with its mistletoe dangling
from the lintel
of our loneliness
and its silver bells tinkling
over the black ice
of bad memories.
And even though
I do not share the Faith,
I welcome the cheer
of hot cider
at the Christmas tree lot
and the drunken colors
of new toys.
For I was once
a red fire truck.
After that,
I adopted the snowman
as my doppelganger
and winter
as my broken sled.
Today is clear and bright,
a tiny locomotive
emerging from the tunnel
of November.
And here—between the stations
of our regret—
the little train
blows a merry note
because we do not

have to carve sin
into the ice floe of religion
to wonder
at the blessed industries
of the North Pole.
Each snowflake
tells a story
that does not require Latin
to decipher.
Each star
shines on Bethlehem.

Einstein's Closet

Pure mathematics is, in its way, the poetry of logical ideas
—Albert Einstein

My wife tells me that Albert Einstein
filled his closet
with identical shirts, slacks and jackets.
You see, he did not want to expend unnecessary energy
coordinating disparate outfits
when there was so much of the cosmos
to explore.
His blackboard was the endless void
of time and space,
and no matter how many atoms of chalk
he scratched onto its surface,
he could never begin to comprehend the totality
of even one of the sequined dinner jackets
that sparkled overhead
on a warm New Jersey night.
When he woke,
there was nothing in his closet
to distract him from the miracle of morning,
or the enormous brain of nature.
He was free to set his hair on fire
with each new epiphany,
or walk the neighborhood,
hands sunk deep into the pockets
of his indistinguishable trousers.
Everything in his world was relative
except for his clothing
which provided some field of unification.
When Albert Einstein opened his closet,
he did not worry about the calculus
of stripes over plaids;

he was too busy humming equations
to himself.
His humble clothes may have looked alike,
but Einstein's closet
altered the study of physics forever
by proving that all things have energy
even when they are resting on their hangers.
And that these rumpled jackets
of energy and mass are interchangeable.
He also proved that it's not the clothes
that make the man—it's the stardust.

While Reading Her Latest Book

I remember the afternoon
this renowned poet
was dragged out of the lake
almost blue with hypothermia.
After a couple of hours,
she'd recovered sufficiently
to laugh at the folly
of trying to swim out so far.
This episode might have been tragic
for American poetry.
But the poet did not perish
in the depths of that alpine lake.
She went back to teaching and writing,
and every once in a while,
one of her poems surfaces
teeth chattering and almost blue
trying to retain its heat
within the cold physics of her loss.
They are the ones
that almost propel themselves
beyond the point of no return.
They fill the margins with her labored breaths.
They carry the watermark of her struggles.
These are the poems I remember,
little gifts regurgitated onto the muddy banks
of some deceptively cold lake.
What I'm trying to say is
that sometimes things work out:
the body remembers that it too
is composed mostly of water.
And that bone chills, heartaches,
percussive fears, and violent dreams

are also susceptible
to the vivifying laws that govern water.
It may not be popular these days
for optimism to bob into view
like a buoy.
In fact, for some, it may be enough
to make these words evaporate.
And yet, I was there that day
on the lake.
I witnessed her recovery.

photo by Charlie Seltzer

Armand Brint

About the Author

Armand Brint received his master's degree in Creative Writing and English from San Francisco State University and has taught Creative Writing at Northern California colleges and universities. He is a popular reader in Mendocino County, California, where he resides, and was the City of Ukiah's first Poet Laureate. Armand's poetry has appeared in many journals; his awards for poetry include the 2013 Jane Reichhold International Prize for Haiku. Armand is the author of two previous books of poetry, *Schools of Light*, Linwood Publishers, 1995 and *The League of Slow Cities*, Tenacity Press, 2001. Armand also co-edited two early books on alternative health practices, the *Holistic Health Handbook*, 1978 and the *Holistic Health Lifebook*, 1981. Armand lives with his wife, Fran, in Ukiah, California.

Acknowledgments

I'd like to thank my wife Fran for her poetical love and encouragement and my son Zachary for allowing me to record his journey. I am grateful to my family and friends for their enthusiastic support. And I'm just plain lucky to live among so many talented writers and to reside in a community that values the arts. I'd also like to thank Lani Kask for her skillful assistance proofing the manuscript and Mary-Ann DeVita Palmieri for her exceptional copy editing. Finally, I'd like to say a special thanks to my editor Marcia Gagliardi, who has been a remarkably perceptive and collaborative reader and poetry enhancer.

I'd also like to espresso thanks to the local cafés that have so often fueled my poems with the bright inspirations of coffee.

Colophon

Poems and captions for *In the Name of Wonder* were set in Gill Sans, which became popular when Cecil Dandridge commissioned Eric Gill to produce Gill Sans in 1929 to be used on the London and North Eastern Railway for a unique typeface for all the LNER's posters and publicity material. Gill Sans was designed to function equally well as a text face and for display.

Titles were set in ITC Kabel, a geometric sans serif typeface designed by German typeface designer Rudolf Koch, and released by the Klingspor foundry in 1927. The face was not named after any specific cable. The name had techy cachet in its day and is primarily metaphorical and allusive, a pun referring to both the monolinear construction of the face and the role of type as a means of communication. Kabel is as much Expressionist as it is Modernist and may be considered as a sans serif version of his 1922 Koch Antiqua, sharing many of its character shapes and proportions, most notably its peculiar *g*. Stroke weights are more varied than most geometric sans-serifs, and the terminus of vertical strokes are cut to a near eight-degree angle.

CPSIA information can be obtained at www.ICGtesting.com
Printed in the USA
BVOW10s2311011013

332594BV00001B/2/P

9 780962 630880